*For Maxine,*
*with Ada ⟨...⟩*

# The Year the Pears Bloomed Twice

Elizabeth Raby

*in friendship,*
*Elizabeth Raby*
*12/14/14*

D0760495

Copyright © 2009 Elizabeth Raby
cover photo by Katia Mitova
interior illustration by Steven Schroeder

VIRTUAL ARTISTS COLLECTIVE
http://vacpoetry.org
ISBN: 978-0-9798825-7-9

"A Life of Greed" was published as a broadside by the Mulberry Poets and Writers Association. "Legacies" appeared in *The Ice Man*, and "The Stone" in *Yarrow*. Versions of "A Life of Greed," "Summer Night," "Avarice," "The Pleasures of Landscape," "Cupidity as Torture," "Early Crossing," "Waking Up Two Mornings in a Row," "Legacies," "Quiet Women," "Mother," "The Stone," "Sojourner," "Rabbits," "The Anachronism," and "The Orange" were published in *The Hard Scent of Peonies*, Jasper Press, 1990. Versions of "Prudery is a Form of Avarice," "Desire," "Rondel," "Spoils" (previously titled "Victory"), "Memorial Day," "To New Parents," "Summer Solstice," "I Would Have You There for One Whole Day," "House," "September 10 in the Year of the Twice-Blooming Pears," "September 20," and "Flames" were published in *Camphorwood*, Nightshade Press, 1992. Some of the same poems had appeared previously in *Creeping Bent, I Know, The Journal of New Jersey Poets,* and *Potato Eyes.* "Romance," "Two Weeks in 1948," "Tables," "Drumbeat," "Primate Behavior," "For My Daughter at Fifteen," "6 PM, Hotel Colon," "From the Garden of Earthly Delights," "Asymptotes to the Hyperbole," "Ten Degrees Above Zero," "Neighbors at the River," "Excerpt from a Letter Berthe Morisot Might Have Written to Edouard Manet," and "Ritual" were published in *Ten Degrees Above Zero*, Jasper Press, 2005. "Neighbors at the River," "For My Daughter at Fifteen," "Pride and Glory," and "Ritual" were published in *Manzanita Quarterly.* "Asymptotes to the Hyperbola" and "And Still They Come" appeared in *US 1 Worksheets.* "From the Garden of Earthly Delights" appeared in *The Journal of New Jersey Poets.* "Chatting" appeared in *Santa Fe Literary Review.* "Margins" and "Rabbits" were on the CD, *Poets for Peace, Vol. 1,* from Authentic Voice Records. "The Gritty Old Dog" appeared in *Sin Fronteras/Writers Without Borders.*

*With thanks and deepest appreciation to Steven Schroeder, Katia Mitova, and Patricia Goodrich...*

*for Christopher Bursk, inspiration, mentor, friend...*

# Table of Contents

## One

## Two

## Three

## Four

# One

# A Life of Greed

There was the early and unreasonable
passion for my yellow and white cat.
His death day fell to pieces around me
and, after that, no day ever
fully assembled.

But I found thick frost
on the window at the foot of the stairs
and learned to step through
white ferns, crystal trees
to the place behind them.
In the street I discovered
feathers of ice that concealed
a great river running along the curb.

In the summer I slipped
into the nightrub and sway
of the maples outside my window.
In the garden I found the hard scent
of peonies, the black kingdom
at the heart of the tulip.
I learned the shock of lake water and,
down under the water,
the silent world of weedy sand.

Then I discovered young men,
the amazing number of them,
their hazardous imperfect beauty.
And next, the warm weight of babies,
milky snuffles and grunts against my breast,
and the taste of small knees,
the speedy beat of small hearts.
It was never enough.

In a white cottage in Cornwall there was a bed
shadowed by thatch and fat roses.
The room was full of the sound of bees
and the casual bell of a goat.

And there was a door one block from the Arno
that opened to the accumulating exultant
echo of Monteverdi. A solid man in a white apron
charged only for the wine poured
from the huge new bottle. His wife grilled
pork chops on fresh sage. On a tall cabinet,
potatoes and green beans cooled in glass bowls.
And still I want more.

# Summer Night

### I.

I linger in the heat of the water, washing
cups and plates. Through the window
the overwhelming scent of phlox.
The blooms are luna moths against the humid black.
I want, in this sweet soup of night, your
thick arms and furred chest against me.
And yet still I want to trace with my fingers
the swollen warmth of his palm. I want his hands
on my body. I want to lie with him.

### II.

The two men have gone somewhere. She and I finish
our drinks. In the starless air she
is soft phosphorescence. Tonight
a harem would seem the proper setting
even if we were not the prince's favorites,
had never once been called. Still
we would slip from scented water;
we would brush each other's hair, rub
oils into our calves, between each finger,
be brought melon by the eunuchs, draw delicate
silks across our bellies, our breasts.

# Cupidity as Torture

Miss Grace taught history in tight skirts,
her legs apart, rocking her pelvis
into the corner of her desk, massaging
her throat, her shoulders, the top of her breasts.
We looked away, embarrassed.

Lillie left her husband to groan with a man
who put her on the street. She worked it,
a novelty in her gray coat, pink hat
with blue flowers, a little veil. Now she walks
bent, white, rouged.

Why fill me with this need to root and rut,
to put so much at risk?

## Legacies

If  had joined the State Department instead
of becoming a lady, perhaps I would
have written memos. Because I always
had lady-like tendencies,  I would have
worked hard to reconcile opposing opinions.
I would exist in State as the creature
of someone else's imagination.

In 1899 Kate Chopin wrote
about a woman who awoke
and, discovering there was no room
for her, swam away.

Today I would choose to swim away:
the sky is a perfect blue.
Still duty restrains me; any legacy but that.
I remember my mother's narrow feet,
swollen fingers, purple bows, twin
birthmarks on her shoulders.

# Desire

I've always been careful
to have a man's desire
be greater than my own
that no one be hurt
that I be safe
now each day explodes
out of the day before
this thing I have constructed
in my head becomes some yearning
so vast it takes over my body
settles painfully in my sex
if you do not want it
kill it

# The Pleasures of Landscape

I.

This morning air:
   The friend who doesn't move to a different town.
   The mother with no expectations.
   The delicate touch of the other lover, the one I
   never had.
As always, this air touches my skin,
   the backs of my knees, the flesh
   above my elbow, my hands.
It is easier to love the air
   than it is to love you.
This air gives itself endlessly.


II.

The other lover:
   From four feet away,
   I give you everything.
   I spend myself
   at your back.
   Almost is probably brilliant,
   doesn't carry a knife,
   loves me most of all.
   Never having is delicious,
   constant.

# Early Crossing

Two cats, one orange, one gray, sit on the snowcrust,
five feet apart, facing the river.
They adjust their skins.
With perfect attention, their heads turn
to every sound.

Bank of broken cattails and vines like skeins of wire,
beautiful as the orderly corn stubble across the road.

I hear the cheerful chink, chink
of the chains on passing cars.

Blue shadows, faint sky, yellow light.

Fine crust of ice at the river's edge.

Cold water fills my boots.

## Avarice

Yesterday we sat behind our window
with toast and coffee.

Four deer browsed under the apple trees,
slow and calm as cattle.

Now in this pale drizzle, stripped,
I stand under the shower
shielded a bit
by the trees' bent branches and wormy fruit.

I hope the rain has kept our neighbor
inside today with his high-powered rifle,
his range finder,
but as the water steams over
the brown, the white, the fur of my body,
I don't care.

I want this pouring heat
as we lie on the deep grass, the rotten
fruit and stinging yellow jackets
until we slip through the mud into the dark below
until I cannot tell where the earth
of your body or my body
or the yellow jackets
or the soft apples
divide

# Waking Up Two Mornings in a Row

First Day:

It's enough that she lives
with me. Now she visits my dreams as well.
I had wanted to kill her.

I assumed she would die
if I left her there
without food and water,
and that, after awhile, I wouldn't remember
her anymore.
                        One day even
after all these years she was
tapping on the attic floor again.
I didn't have the energy not to think
about her, so I decided to let her out.

She's been down here
for a couple of years now.
Not at all what I expected –
so ordinary – she, too, is afraid
of the telephone, and she eats
far too much. She wastes hours
pretending. Full of these
embarrassing longings
(that evidently she's willing to tell
to anybody,)
she's all lust, all need.

Second Day:

I wake having spent the night
in a weaving line of people.
We were weary for a shower
or warm soup or somewhere
to lie down, but all night
we left our places to tell
from one to the other along the line,
our shabby stories, bright schemes.
All of us moved slowly
in the same direction.

## "Prudery is a Form of Avarice"

the fortune cookie says. A bored writer's
bad joke?  Perhaps the factory employs
newly arrived relatives to find words
at random in the Chinese/English dictionary.
Then again, in Chinese, "prudery" may have
another meaning; "avarice" is something else
entirely than the insatiable desire
that once again races across this salted field,
this ruined battleground, this history
of hope, my body, that wants you.
My need, hidden in the dead propriety
of dried hummocks, old haystacks,
muddy furrows, is never answered.
It remains a prig to greed.

## Pride and Glory
*For William Coble*

Stillness:
an enormous black box
stolid on three legs.
A man seated before it
begins to play
the row of white keys
fringed in black.
The room fills
with a wash of sound
that eddies out
beneath his supple hands.

Reminds her of another
man's story; his delight
in discovery that if he
touched a woman just so,
used his hands
like this, like that,
he could produce
sounds, a ripple,
that for a moment
filled the world.

# Rondel

White and black,
snowy day,
winter tree,
a round of three
female cardinals.

Three orange dagger beaks,
three breasts, three backs,
gray green, subtle
ornaments of yellow,
fancy swords, red,
on six wings.

Flutter, thrust,
parry around two
still points:
one scarlet male,
one full feeder.

Two never do
attain their desires.
A decoration staged for one
hungry god who draws
a casual parallel.

# Two

# Bird Life

Short, scrappy, free?
No. Compulsion drives
the chickadee too. He
examines the birdhouse,
in, out, in, out, even as
snow buries its green roof
in white.

The male house finch
pursues his lady through
shrieking wind
and blowing sleet. Nothing
dissuades him.

Do the female chickadee,
the lady finch see beauty
in the bright courting feathers
of their pursuers,

take pleasure in the agile flight
and flirtation of their
would-be mates?  To think
dinosaurs have come

to this:
       a movement in the leaves,
       a flash of yellow,
       a haunting song.

# From the Garden of Earthly Delights

A thick green hornworm moves
its many lime-flesh feet across
the tomato plant's top branch.
A load of white menhir bristles
its back; eggs laid to hatch
and feed on green skin, green
jelly guts, make it visible.
Perhaps if this wrinkled length
were the first I had seen,
I could admire the cool symmetry,
vegetable disguise. But such creatures
filled Grandfather's garden, and I
had to squash the leather bodies
one after another. I do it again today
but, for the most part, this garden,
laid out years ago when I could
work on my knees, gives more
than I can use, excuses to dig,
to dawdle, to watch. This morning
a yellow-throated warbler's
*wichity-wichity;* the close circling
of a turkey buzzard; twin fawns
who nudge their mother, are pushed
away, settle for fallen apples.
A baby robin flaps and falls,
branch to branch, awkward
in the maple tree, while its family
fights the mockingbird who comes
to close. I watch from the easy
distance I like best.

25

# Collaterals

She was going to write another poem
about the birds in her yard, the goldfinch vivid
at the feeder, the male's yellow breast
and black back, the red-breasted nuthatch
and the chickadees investigating the junipers,
mention perhaps the bold flock of gray jays
feasting on fallen pinion nuts, the return
yesterday of winter visitors, juncos
and white-crowned sparrows, but then
it occurred to her to wonder about the birds
of Iraq, species unknown to her, their fate.
She hopes a quiet garden is hidden somewhere
in Baghdad behind a sheltering wall, that
a woman there has found enough water
for a few pots of bright flowers, tangled
vines, and a moment's surcease from worry
about her family, the sounds of guns, sirens,
breaking glass, the stench of rising smoke.
Perhaps the woman is remembering a time
she drank tea at a table in the shade,
enjoying the birds' bright flit and dart,
their brave songs, their miraculous flight.

# Spoils

This burnt smell
makes it hard to breathe.
I stand guard at the border.
Sudden echoes startle
me. I raise my gun,
but it is only
the report of metal sheets
folded and torn, suddenly sprung free
as scavengers dig for something useful
over there;
  their bent forms are wary,
far apart from one another.
  They pick through piles of rubbish, burnt,
so, at this distance, they all appear to be one thing,
enormous, heavy and gray, like rock.

That sound
brings to mind
my first *Tenebrae,*
the altar shrouded in purple cloth;
everything still, lights
extinguished one by one
until it was so dark
I couldn't see anything,
not even my mother next to me.
Then a terrible sound,
thunder, inside, directly above me,
or many horses galloping
over hard ground. She told me
it was only the janitor
up in the bell tower
rattling a cookie sheet,
but I was relieved when someone
brought a candle.

27

The wind comes up like this every afternoon.
The scavengers dig; the mounds groan and collapse.
I wonder if those wisps that rise around them
are ashes, blowing, or if some of the debris
on that side is still on fire.

28

# Memorial Day

Coals in the grill. A trick
of sun and breeze and flag;
transparent stripes, red and white, drift
across the patio. At the end
of this hidden lane, we never lock our doors.

      In a quiet forest
          diggers
                arrange rows of skulls,
                    broken teeth,
        along the top of the pits.


    Outside the stone walls, relatives say
    it is not possible to hear the screams.


Once there was a park
              until men in rubber aprons
    used hooks to pull naked bodies
              from the trucks.

    He said – ten minutes in any building
        and I've found a place to hide –
    They found him in his bed.

Boys pressed into the sand
   as it exploded around them.
A few begged for water.

        Kneeling before him,
           the king's first wife
           attached a thorn to a rope
           and pulled it through her tongue

to sanctify
the birth of the second wife's son.

Birds with pointed tails circle
the pitted limestone well, *cenote.*
From its walls, maiden skulls peer up
through chalky water.
How close to the edge
did they go believing?
Dressed, praised and adored,
the center of attention.
The moment before
the heart was removed.

30

## To New Parents

Never say his name.
Don't speak the words out loud.
You mustn't bring him to the notice
of those who keep the records.

When you feel the wind upon your back
never look his way.

Don't let them see the marks he makes in you,
and when joy breaks you, whisper joy to him,
tight in your arms, under a tight roof.

Don't dance under the sky.
Don't draw the lightning down.

## In the Guarnaci Etruscan Museum, Volterra, Italy

This blade of a boy, two feet high,
twenty-two hundred years old, stands
in his glass cage, his face, a well-loved
pleasant face one might see today
on the steep streets of Volterra, full lips
held in an enigmatic half smile
beneath a broad nose,
hair parted on the left, ear length,
neatly waved across his forehead. He looks
at us directly. He is not afraid.

*L'Ombra della Sera,* d'Annunzio named him,
Shadow of the Evening, because the little
bronze figure is elongated as though he were
his own shadow cast by a setting sun.

Below his chin the naked body begins
its thin stretch, three or four times
ordinary proportions. The boy's hips
tilt slightly to the right. He holds
his arms against his body, his hands
clasp bare thighs, legs press together,
ten toes spread firm and still. Who was he?
Who is he to pull at us so?
Although this slender stake
is formed like no boy who ever lived,
he is alive all the same.

# Boy

Boy with white wings .
sprouting from his back
rides his bicycle up the sky.
Grandmother is angry, shakes
her broad red fist at him –
Come home!  Come back!
It is too soon. Who will fetch
water for me, bring wood? –
He smiles, his small white teeth
gleam in the sun – Good-bye, he
laughs, Good-bye – his wheels
whirl toward thick moist cloud,
tips of his quivering wings
the last things to disappear.

His Baba stirs lonely soup,
sweeps the clean hearth,
damps down the last
carnelian glow of fire.

She herself has never flown,
never felt the tug and lift
of wings on her back.

Gray stockings rolled down
to the tops of worn black shoes,
she has been too busy knitting,
shelling peas. What more did
they want from her, she wonders.

The boy rose and rose until
there was only God, but God
had turned his back on him.
The boy wanted to see God's

face but God did not turn,
He only was. The boy flashed
his wings in anger. With all his
little strength, he pushed
God into His vault and
slammed the clouds on him.

Baba looked up at the last
lightning, heard the last thunder,
the final roar and render
of the sky. For an instant
she remembered her boy,
his bicycle, the beginning
of his jaunty ride.

# Summer Solstice

In Virginia today the air is full of angels,
the upper parts of their bodies Madonna blue.
They fly pulled upright by the weight
of voluminous skirts of trailing gauze.
Pairs of transparent wings beat fast.

Caught and put on my palm, one is half the size
of my smallest fingernail. She seems relieved
to rest. Tempted to keep her, I am afraid
to risk it. I let her go.

She hovers above a honeysuckle entangled
in the top of a boxwood. One strand
of the slender vine is suddenly alive.
The snake darts out and seizes her
in its grass-green mouth.

# Poet-in-the-School

Yesterday a girl chose
a two-sided stone
from my rainbow bag.
She imagined the rough ugly side
lay exposed; the beautiful side
was buried in sand. People stepped
on the stone, pushed it down
deeper and deeper.

Her name is Grace. She's tangled
and dark. If she weren't
in the sixth grade room, if she stood
ahead of me in the check-out line
at 7-Eleven, I would see her,
if I saw her at all, not as a girl
of twelve, but as a grown woman,
short, pretty, dirty and tired.
I would imagine, if I bothered
to imagine, a man waiting outside,
sullen in a dark green Crown Victoria
shouting at streaky children
who tumble in the back seat.

Today her poem said
people think she's mean
but really she's kind.
People think she's dirty
but really she has pretty clothes.
People think she doesn't care
but really she does.

Her handwriting is clear.
Her spelling is almost perfect.

36

# The Gritty Old Dog

follows his boy
down the sidewalk,
stops to examine
every mailbox,
every departing squirrel,
every tree. From
gray-streaked muzzle
to white-tipped tail,
his black body,
still sturdy
but lopsided,
is given in service
to this walk.
His right front paw,
withered, twisted,
raised, permanently
points toward
the next moment,
next hour, next
adventure
of this dog's
ardent life.

## On the Train – 1958

Once, a long time ago, a young woman
got on the train. She knew who
would meet her. The sheets on her bed
would be cold. She knew the sound
every door in the house made
closing, and how long it took
before the water ran hot in the sinks.
As usual there would be
a small fir tree in the corner
of the living room. Her mother would grind
oranges and cranberries together and put them
in cut glass.

The woman sat next to an old man
with a German accent who rested his head
against the back of his seat.
He told her he was tired
from his trip to Israel.
He had gone to search
until he found at least someone
who had survived.
He had discovered
a second cousin once removed.
Together they had remembered,
but now he was returning to Albany
which he preferred. It had less past.
He wept. The woman wept with him.

The train reached Albany.
Frail as he was he insisted that
he carry her bag. Free
to leave this train,
they stood on the platform.
He held out his hand,
a lonely geology of bones and veins.
She clasped it in her own
still soft with inexperience.

# Three

## Quiet Women

there once was a quiet woman
who went to a lecture
where she heard a man speak
from inside his lecture the man
called to her, beneath his words
she heard him say
you, you, you, I could know you
and in time he did
and they had a daughter
who heard the story, who forgot the story
even forgot the mother
the daughter suffered and prospered
and lived many years listening
to the sound of her own voice in her head
one day she went to a lecture
where she heard a man speak
from inside his lecture the man
called to her, beneath his words
she heard him say
you, you, you, I could know you
so she sent him a message in code
you, you, you, I could know you
he heard the woman and then
she remembered the story
and her mother and relearned
suffering and was glad

# I Would Have You There for One Whole Day

It would be summer, the windows open,
green scent and birdsong
suffusing the room. Goldenrod
from the meadow in a blue vase,
slouched leather of old chairs,
polished wood.

*Is it a mistake, this day?*
*There's a small ache*
*at my center. I don't know*
*if others have it. I've been afraid*
*to ask. Sometimes it grows until*
*I become its center, as it has now*
*that I'm sitting here with you.*

*Look out there at the meadow*
*sloping down to the pond, the dark hill*
*reflected in the pond, the mountains.*
*This range of faded blue*
*always meant home to me.*
*I'm not here often.*

*Once I saw in the cathedral in Toledo*
*the hats of old cardinals hanging*
*high on a thread. Their souls can't*
*fly to heaven until the hats fall.*
*It has not happened.*

43

## Romance

Compulsive rummages
through Mother's dark
mahogany dresser, its
narrow middle drawer
lined in pale wood –
folded handkerchiefs,
patterned linen and Swiss lace,
one of silk chiffon, its lilies
of the valley, purple pansy, tied
with a curling ribbon of blue,
worked in tiny cross-stitch.
Beneath them all, a bottle
of Chanel No. 5, crystal-
stoppered, sent by her sailor
brother from far Paree.
The unused scent, the whisper
of chiffon clinging to my probing
fingers – the beautiful secret
mother I desired.

44

# Two Weeks in 1948

A shale cliff above the lake – a compound of spacious
screened-porch summer houses – our cottage the poor

relation, a dim room set on cement blocks, an island
in a pond of garter snakes that created its own

weather, an endless undulation of trillium and ferns,
the roil and boil of coiling waves – a raised path of beaten

grass our bridge across their mass. Four cots, a folding table
and chairs, a camp stove, a kerosene lamp could not

have kept Mother busy, but only once do I remember her
with us on the beach, pale and awkward in a limp wool suit.

What did she do while we played cards on the porches
where the other women smoked, sipped long summer drinks,

gossiped on musty kapok lounges?  I see her, in an apron
edged in rickrack, a housedress she had made herself,

sweeping the bare floor. Summer leisure forever foreign
to her nature, never at home in the life she achieved.

## Mother

Father had done the best
he could do, put up a card table
in the guest room beside her bed,
leased a telephone
for thirty days, and put it there
for her, but the room looked sparse,
temporary, and she a stranger to it.
She's not eating, he told me,
she hardly sleeps.
He was bewildered
that after all these years
she should want to sleep alone.
I went to work. Every meal
I set the tray with her polished silver,
roses in the white jade vase,
crisp embroidered napkins
from the camphorwood chest.
She ate perfect poached eggs,
salmon mousse, sugar cookies,
the edges an even brown,
applesauce made with the skins
but milled smooth. She could pretend
I was what she wanted. I knew
all her recipes for a graceful life.
For a few days, they eased us both.

# A Congregational Viewing in Vermont, 1970

Father wanted the viewing
because people would expect it.

We sat before Mother's open coffin.
I can't remember what she wore –
something special she had put by
for the occasion. I could only see
her face and her fingers,
a yellow translucence without
their living beat of blood.

People shook our hands, kissed
our cheeks. My granite mouth
managed to emit words that said
nothing again and again.

My young African friend remained with us
until at last the coffin closed. Then he
whispered to me:
>Why is no one weeping?
>Did you not love your mother?

He could not know the effort, the absurd
effort, not to seize the wax dummy she
had become, to call her to come back, mutinous
phlegm and water disfiguring my stone face.

47

# Drumbeat

Free to roam one square block
but never, never, to cross
a street, I felt the thum, thum

in my feet and ran to the corner
to watch it come. Now came girls
with silver batons spinning up

to the sun and behind them
neat blue ranks of measuring legs
and the steady beat and the thum,

thum, thum of the enormous drum.
Thum, thum, thum, my three steps
to the band's every one,

along the block to the magic curb –
but the thum went on and on and
pulled me across that street

and then another and then another
until the band stood still to play
its songs while the thum in my feet

attached to a fear in my belly and, sure
enough, there was my father come
to find me. On the lawn before the band

he spread me across his knees, and facing
the music, I learned shame from giving way
to the beat of the luring drum.

# The Stone

The stone is oblong with white streaks,
a marbling of fat in meat,
lamb perhaps, because one side
is rough, opaque as the fell
left on the lamb
after the wool is stripped away.

The color is not the color of meat
but of milk and butterscotch,
or of the graham crackers drizzled
with honey and milk my father
ate at night in the kitchen in Vermont
sitting alone at the white table,
or of the apricot jam he bought
in Beirut by the five pound jar
to spread on fine-textured French bread.

The texture of the stone
is like nothing living, hard, cool,
clear to the depths on two sides,
reassuring, something to roll in the hand,
like one from the string of worry beads
he bought and carried behind him,
he, a tall Swede with hairy knuckles
and strong hands, turning the smooth stones
as he walked daily through the *souks*,
a beret over his fine straight hair.
His eyes behind receding spirals
of gold-rimmed glasses as eager
as a hawk's above his incurving
beak of a nose.

49

Beirut was still Paris of the Middle East
then, a zesty stewpot of lamb and thyme
simmering on cedar logs brought down
from the mountains. It was still years
until my father's stomach sealed itself
and he starved without complaint in a quiet bedroom
in Jericho, Vermont, only able to cast out
strings of yellow mucous into the white enamel
pot brought down specially from the attic.

His beautiful massive bones, elegant
against the white sheets, gradually
superseding the daily starbursts
of blue and purple veins, the yellow flesh
turned superfluous, shining, hard.

# Primate Behavior

The little animal in her arms roots,
desperate, along the hairless breast,
flexes tiny digits, snorts, finds
the tender nipple. A moment's pain,
the milk lets down, carries
the mother to a warm night
in a leaf nest.
She wants nothing –
the world is a steady sucking.
Small grunts, tongue clicks,
the infant head slips from the nipple,
snores, starts, snores again.
Blue milk dribbles from the corner
of its half-open mouth.

## 6 PM, Hotel Colon
## Cathedral Square
## Barcelona, Spain

It appears so comfortable
spread out to view
in a yellow glare of light.
The belly pulls down
in strained folds
to a dark tag of hair below.
The waist slips
from the center of the body
to rest in two soft handfuls
on the white sheet.

Perhaps the torso sprawls on white sheets
by its window every day,
to be fed sandwiches from a plate
beside the pillow, to lift newspapers
on and off its bosom with lazy hands.
Or is it a special treat,
a holiday from all expectations
other than its own?

From behind concealing shutters
my daughters and I watch
the pages turn across the flesh,
fingers swish a box of tissues
in and out of sight, scratch
a desultory scratch. The girls giggle,
cannot look away. I watch them
watching this ease about the body
I can't provide.

52

# For My Daughter at Fifteen

Your walls are covered with posters
of ambiguous boys, whole bands
who look like you –
smooth, beautiful, distant.

Today you tell me a boy insisted
he knows your friends,
the things they like to do with him,
where they let him put it
and where they don't,
what they say.

You aren't hungry,
go to your room. All evening
you play your wildest music.

In the morning you come to breakfast
with shoulders back, shirt tucked in,
the inverted heart of your buttocks
clear beneath your jeans.

But when the bus comes,
you hunch yourself, pull your shirt
free, have nothing to do
with your body.

53

# Margins

In the middle of our old field
I was surprised to discover
the doe, so close and still.
Her body spoke desire
for the woods, but her head
was turned back
over her shoulder to watch me.
I took three steps. The doe
held her ground. I stopped;
she stood. I took another step;
she spoke. Five feet ahead of me
two fawns, spotted, but already
skilled at leaps and bounds
zig-zagged to meet her.

The next day as we sat
by the pond, the fawns,
no taller than the Queen Anne's
lace from which they edged,
twitched onto the lawn –
the beginning of a long summer
of delinquent behavior. The doe,
nervous in the woods, whistled
her haunted warnings.

A mother, I know my mother's
caution. A daughter, I know
my daughter's impatience. Myself,
I know nothing is safe.

# House

There was a house full of windows,
closets and drawers, people who needed.

A housewife lived in the house,
lived by the windows, by the stew on the stove,

forgot the start of the story,
about the babies, the things broken and repaired.

She told her daughter, whom she loved,
to find a life beyond the windows,

not to do what she had done.
But the housewife wondered what,

beyond the windows, was the life that meant
more than these people, their need.

# Sojourner

It is something small, despite the great thwack,
that plummets down the window to the cement.
A heap of black and white, wings angled,
black needle-beak open, heaving gasps.
The beak closes and then the eyes;
the body continues to shake from the effort
of breath. Is the left wing broken?
It fans out motionless.

I get my *Field Guide.*
A black and white warbler,
but the stripes of this back
are not so regular, the white borders
of the tail more distinct,
the lines on this breast softer,
the wings a deeper black.
The thick black feathers on this head
flare elegantly around center white.
Five inches seems smaller
than I would have guessed.

Eyes still closed, the warbler works
its wings gradually against its body,
a neat package listing slightly to the left.
Its breathing steadies. The black eyes open,
blink, clear and brighten, begin
to follow my movements behind the window,
their expression almost my expression.

My dog comes to stand beside me,
sees the small injury, barks. A sudden flash
of black and white. From the maple tree,
the warbler scolds softly, sings a tentative
*weese, weese, weese, weese, weese, weese, weese.*
Such a long journey ahead
and already in trouble.

## Rabbits

For two years now rabbits have built
a nest in the garden's thick mulch,
a hop away from the row of beets,
the fresh sweet greens. I could have told them
life was not meant to be so simple –
easy lettuce has a price.
I didn't mean to find them – an uprooted
weed, then sudden surprising movement,
frightened cries.

I would have shared my garden; an idea
they could not understand. The first time
they were large enough to scatter, panicked,
injuring themselves against the fence
we thought would keep them out. This year
a squirming gray-brown bunch. I cover them
but the cats dig them out one by one. A long
dispiriting process. Is this how God sees us?
Screams – loud and troubling –
but nothing to be done.

# September 10 in the Year of the Twice-Blooming Pears

My old dog and I make a late start:
the sky still sharp blue, the few clouds
that section the sky, bronze.
It is cold tonight. We walk
by the pear trees whose leaves
have dropped early to reveal
scattered fruit and scabby branches
tipped by bits of white bloom,
like birds held at the feet, trapped
butterflies, pinned cabbage moths –
strange accents in a landscape
of goldenrod and aster.

In the garden, Caesar groans
as he folds his legs on still warm straw.
Marigolds, amaranth, zinnias over the edge
of excess. Our strange tomatoes, orange
like giant persimmons, drop from the vines.
Green peppers bend their plants.
Frost is predicted. I gather all I can.
Caesar barks and there at the top
of a pear tree, above white blossoms
and a few newly hatched red leaves,
is an owl. He lifts off, a soundless
ghost, and flies into the swamp.

# September 20

Last week, in perfect weather, we
had a wedding here. The bride and groom
stood just there. There were flowers
everywhere, in the bride's arms
and on her head and on the white-clothed
tables under the white tent where we ate
a pig carved down to not much but his ribs,
his leather face, his radish eyes. If he
is dug up someday, perhaps they will wonder
who roasted him whole and ate him. They won't
know it was the year the pears bloomed twice.

# Four

# Neighbors at the River

Parked cars appear to have been
tarred and feathered overnight

by rain and falling leaves.
Yesterday the man across the street

pulled his tomato plants and leaned
the stakes against each other

as though he were preparing
a bonfire. This morning, water streams

over his orange zinnias, brown
at the stems, fat dahlias, stalks

of white foxglove left to die and dry
in their own time. He has been friendly –

all the neighbors have been friendly –
a welcoming word, a handshake, warnings

about each other and the river. *That one*
just released from jail again. Don't speak

to *his* wife or he'll be after you.
*Those two* have an addict for a mother.

The drugs got into the little one's brain.
If one morning your tires have nails

in them look in *that* direction
Keep your doors locked.

Always run your sump pump. Has the river
risen in your basement yet?

Below the levee, the river, gray
and flat, swallows the rain.

## Still They Come

The scurry and scratch
of mice in the walls.
She imagines
a sudden hole,
the fall
of tiny bodies,
scrambling
wet fur
in her coffee cup,
delicate feet
seeking traction
in a plate
of rice and beans,
whiskers probing
her pillow, her
cheek. A dark gleam
slips beneath the gate,
darts to the rug
at the door,
eats the fringe
strand by strand.
The rug itself
seems to dissolve.
Microscopic teeth
busy all night.

# Hummingbird Wars

A sharp edge to the morning warns
it won't be long. Killing cold comes early
at this altitude. This garden would shock
my disciplined grandmother. Here in
the semi-desert, any native or colonizer
that blooms is welcome, no matter how wild
or disorderly – Apache plume, Indian paint brush,
Mexican hat, blanket flower, cholla cactus,
sunflower, blue mist spirea, potentilla,
Russian sage, rayless gumweed, rabbitbush –
a messy profusion hospitable to all our
summer birds. Despite the flowers and three
full feeders, twenty or thirty hummingbirds,
furies at the sugar water, fly off to challenge
each other in aggressive soars and dives.
Their industrious wings beat eighty times
a second, their long tongues furl in nectar
from pink and yellow tubes of the honeysuckle's
frantic second bloom. Soon the hummingbirds,
pugnacious bits of iridescence, will spark their way
two thousand miles to shrinking winter battlegrounds.

## Flames

Generous rows of closed
red and yellow tulips lean
toward the snow as if
they had made an embarrassing mistake
and could now think only
of covering themselves.
The photograph is undated,
yellowed, or perhaps the sky
was yellow that day and the air
as well. In the middle distance
snow has transformed the stone
of the outdoor fireplace
into something strange –
an abandoned chimney left
after a settler's farm had burned,
or perhaps a ruined tank.
Beyond it, snow-plastered trunks,
whitened branches of evergreens.
Finally a dim mass of woods.
In fact, I don't remember the day at all.

Today is clear and bright, the snow
melting, but still deer tracks are distinct
on the path. My old dog sniffs at them.
His huge paws move steadily despite
uncertain hips. His happiness with each
familiar root and stump on this
familiar walk never wears out. His joy
is apparently the last thing to go.

So many snow scenes – a few weeks ago
I looked out across Central Park at immense
gray clouds in a white sky, gray rectangles
of buildings against the clouds, the twisted

geometry of bare branches and twigs contained
within the pillowy height of trees, a thin
cover of snow on the grass. On bare asphalt
paths, pre-schoolers, snow-suited balls of blue,
fuchsia, yellow and orange, scattered and rolled
like un-racked billiard balls.

I pick out the beauty, make up
its meaning. The people I read about
who experienced near death hovered
close to the ceiling, seeing their bodies,
the busy nurses, the stunned relatives,
but then, this time, they came back
to say that death is not death. A gift
to ease us into the winds perhaps:
the Matchgirl's bright flame.

# Dreaming a Headline
*Dead Woman Wakes Wearing a Bracelet from Heaven*


From the cloud of her cotton nightdress
she stretches painful arms and is
surprised by the hard sound one
makes against the headboard, unfamiliar

clunk of metal and stone. She lowers
a heavy wrist before her newly
opened eyes and discovers strands
of braided gold – yellow, white, and rose –

each burdened by jewels, by lapis
lazuli, fire opal, topaz, turquoise,
by angel skin coral, aquamarine.
She turns her hand this way and that,

weighs the bracelet's delicate slap
and drape on her hanging skin,
brittle bones. Back from the long tunnel
of light, the welcoming arms, to this

everyday ache of gut, the bilious green
of morning, the fevered yellow nights. One
flash of sun finds its way beneath the shade,
illumines the facets of this cryptic gift.

## For Dorothy,
## at eighty-three hoping for a speedy end

I wish you could sit with me today
here on this shaded *portal*.

Pull leaves from the basil plant
to release its sharp green scent.

Watch the wren and his hopeful tail
disappear beneath the spirea's blue mist.

Enjoy the stories the clouds carry
in their progress across bright autumn sky.

Tell me again your story, and his.
If only for a moment, let the buzz

and chatter of hummingbirds
ease your stumbling heart.

69

## Asymptotes to the Hyperbola

Imagining a blind man imagining blue
moving out along a branch
of the curve of great sky that for him
is only the feel of air touching his skin.
Would he in compensation feel gravity's weight
bearing down on him outside and always,
as I am only when I pull against it, as when
first one black-shod foot and then the other
climbs the risers of scarred orange heart-pine?

Red – I think I could not live without red,
but red is only one gift. Without the pepper's glow
I could turn to something else: the tiny hum
of the refrigerator, the pressure of cup against
my lips, the stale air in this room. No! If I had
his senses, I would not put up with this air
one minute more. I would open the door to wisps
of cold, the cat's quiet greeting, the sun's
reaching warm to my hair from the unseen
there open above me.

# Ten Degrees above Zero

Clumps of ice clot the steel flow
of cold river. Below this bridge
the lost sole of a boot,
crumpled aluminum, a truck tire,
rest, foreshortened in clear
winter water. The swallows' nests
are silent, flaking in the wind.
In a gray sky, one yellow streak
hangs at the horizon. A multitude
of geese paddle between bristled banks
on water the sluggish silver of mercury.
Geese feet and bodies strain upstream,
while their heads curl backwards
over long necks to see where, against
their desire, the river takes them.

That first January, the Cuban refugees,
suckered into heatless houses, steam
rising from water they boiled for warmth,
saw the leafless branches, the brown grass,
and were afraid green was lost to them
forever. Still they endured, even danced
the *meringue* to heat cold floors. They
had learned to hope against reason.

# The Orange

*For Carolyn Forché*

There is no irony in an orange.

Last night a poet forced her to think
about this world; how someone can find
an excuse for almost every horror.
She wonders if the mind's dangerous search
for that grand narcotic, meaning,
is the origin of irony.

Today, for the first time, she thinks
about an orange.

The womb of her mind has sometimes opened
eagerly, sometimes been forced
to take in misshapen or perfect remnants
of the wisdom of her time.

She decides the hint
of a guiding intelligence
rests in the black humor
of being a seed case that desires
to mean more.

The orange is young, firm and muscular
in her hand. Peeled and torn apart
the fruit is sweet – its seeds small,
barely formed.

Today she is grateful to the orange
for the orange.

# The Anachronism

This mad need to share the space
inside my head. Last night I touched
the soft spikes of Barrett's baby hair,
put my hands around his velvet heels.
Today a swallow-tail butterfly, blue
with orange spotted under-wings,
landed on white sand next to the pines.

If I could learn to love
the morning accumulation
of shattered glass, smeared paper
against padlocked grates, plastic
drip bags of glucose, the wrinkled bottom
of the old lady, perhaps I could be
as useful to the world as the beauty
I make space for is to me.

A goldfinch, furious beat of bright wings,
challenges the black mirror of the window,
wears himself in impossible desire.

# Ritual

She lusts to connect
bare skin to pool water –
the body entering it, it entering the body –
with a climb in the dark to the top
of this wooden pyramid, this
pink-painted ziggurat turned
luminous gray in the Virginia night.
A nude walk out of the water,
a joggled scaling of the steps.
An eccentric hope for a ritual
to mend some fragment of aging body,
some sadness in the aging brain.
A rehearsal for her return to the elements,
this need for the touch of water and air.

# Ah Provence

This rainy Sunday
I put on my gray sweater,
remember sunshine
on a balcony built over a village wall.
I looked down over red geraniums
tumbled against yellow stone.
In the square, Ives Montand
in white linen, white straw,
bowled with suspendered men
who drank wine from a bottle
and flashed gold teeth. Chagall
rests under a white stone shadowed
by deep cypress. In the shop, two steps
up from the cobblestones, golden soaps
scented with honey and thyme heaped
in baskets; glass vials of lavender oil,
jars of small dark olives packed
in *herbes sauvages*, lined wooden shelves;
wild rosemary filled canvas bags.
In a Saracen cellar, white marble tables,
polished stone floors, a bouquet as big
as a man filled a majestic copper tub.
Odor of lamb, shallots, deep red wine.

But my house is full of dust. There
are ants in the dishwasher, past due
bills on my desk, laundry fills
the hampers, no one's heard from me
in months. Familiar faces fill my head
asking questions I don't want to hear.

# Eclogue:
## Operating at a Loss –
## Expatriates Explain Their Inn

The chateau had been abandoned to dirt and to the owls,
to their night swoops down broad flights of stairs, but we
felt the pull of ancient stories and of escape from our own,
imagined November light, a pale dapple through lace,
the sound of prudent shutters closing, a crystal vase of late
roses, burgundy silk, old wood, polished and restored,

but we bought because of the greenhouse, the curved
segmented roof like a caterpillar's back. It smelled
mossy, damp, like an old flower pot bearded and webbed
with roots. Its ironwork made us think of the Eiffel
tower, of women with bustles strolling beneath
chestnut trees, of green metal tables and prams.

In the market, farmers sell goat cheese, small spheres
stacked in pyramids, newly sprouted lettuce, quail eggs,
each its own tiny arrangement of spots and shades of brown.
We bought because we wanted a long log in the fire, chairs
ringing against the stone floor, conversation at the table. Here
where everything is history, there is no need

to make up for lost time. Perhaps Vercingetorix gathered
acorns under ancestors of that oak. We bought because
of the trees, the oaks, that grove of Douglas fir, this
sequoia, one of two in the whole *Nivernais*. In America,
careless, someone would have cut them out of the way,
sold them or their valuable space.

He sculpts, saws dead branches for the fire. He wires
and plumbs. I cook, wash the linens, trim the roses, write.
We've not lost touch – we work from distance's more
ironical perspective. We've never been able to read a French
train schedule nor the many pages of our deed. Each trip
back we buy the latest books.

We need to have more visitors, sell more work, to make it
last. Listen to the hail beat against the window – so cold.
Arminée heard there will be snow in the mountains tonight.
By morning the last yellow leaves will cover the pond.
I'll make a *pot-au-feu*. Are you ready for a glass of wine?
Still early and almost dark – I do mind these short days.

## Excerpt from a Letter Berthe Morisot Might Have Written to Edouard Manet

I'm not asking you to solve my life.
There is no solution for its rips and tears,
for the tug and tether of those to whom
I am attached, but I wish you could see
that I wrestle with the question of light,
the demands of color, the white of grief and sky
as you do. Our separate lives marked
and measured by faithfulness to what
we save – the moment barely sketched
before the shadows slip –
and by the certain end to sight.

# Chatting

Sixty-three years with never a glimpse
of a chat until this morning. And then
not one, but two; a pair of the big warblers
busy in the stone basin outside
her window. Their assertive splashing kept
even the robins at bay. According to *Sibley*,
chats lurk beneath thick brush year round
in almost every state. She has lived
in several, always with at least a casual eye
on the look-out for anything new. She has
stared out windows, sat motionless
in chairs, walked quietly through woods,
but never before has she spied the chats'
funny white spectacles, olive-gray backs,
white bellies, and bright yellow breasts.

Something fresh just now when so many
of her friends are gravely ill and her own
life has begun to blur. First she forgot
her dreams. Now she loses names, books,
entire days. On her inexorable way out,
perhaps there may still be time to find
yet another bird, or courage, or wisdom,
and by making note, even to remember them.
She must be sure to write it all down.

Elizabeth Raby has been a poet in the schools for the Pennsylvania Council of the Arts, the New Jersey Council of the Arts, and the Geraldine R. Dodge Foundation. She taught poetry writing at Muhlenberg College. She earned a B.A. in History from Vassar College, an M.A. in English (Creative Writing) from Temple University, and is a fellow of the Virginia Center for the Creative Arts. In the summers of 2006 and 2007, Ms. Raby represented the Teachers for Tomorrow program as an English teacher in Deva, Romania. Elizabeth, Patricia Goodrich, and Casandra Ioan collaborated on a bi-lingual poetry collection, *Bone, Flesh & Fur* or *Oase, Carne & Blana*. The poems were translated by Ms. Ioan and published by Petoskey Stone Press. Ms. Raby's other publications include *The Hard Scent of Peonies*, Jasper Press; *Camphorwood*, Nightshade Press; and *Ten Degrees Above Zero*, Jasper Press. She lives in Santa Fe, New Mexico.

LaVergne, TN USA
22 March 2011
220514LV00004B/40/P